Equatorial
& other poems

Also available in this series

Skyquake / Temblor de cielo
Arctic Poems / Poemas árticos
Square Horizon / Horizon carré

Selected Poems

El Cid / Mío Cid Campeador
Cagliostro

Vicente Huidobro

Mirror of Water
Equatorial, Hallali
& Eiffel Tower

El espejo de agua,
Ecuatorial, Hallali
& Tour Eiffel

Translated from Spanish & French by
Eliot Weinberger

Shearsman Books

First published in the United Kingdom in 2019 by
Shearsman Books
50 Westons Hill Drive
Emersons Green
BRISTOL
BS16 7DF

Shearsman Books Ltd Registered Office
30–31 St. James Place, Mangotsfield, Bristol BS16 9JB
(this address not for correspondence)

www.shearsman.com

ISBN 978-1-84861-652-3

The translation of *Eiffel Tower* first appeared
in *The New York Review of Books* in 2014.

El espejo de agua was originally published in Buenos Aires, 1916,
by Biblioteca Orión. It was reissued in Madrid in 1918.

Ecuatorial was originally published in Madrid,
in August 1918, by Imprenta Juan Pueyo.

Hallali, poème de guerre was originally published in Madrid,
1918, by Imprenta Jesús López.

Tour Eiffel was originally published in Madrid, 1918
by Imprenta Juan Pueyo.

The original texts of the poems here are based on those printed in the author's
Obra poética, ed. Cedomil Goic, Paris: ALLCA XX, 2003; the sole exception is
Tour Eiffel, where preference has been given to the spacing employed
in the first edition.

CONTENTS

Vicente Huidobro in 1917 and 1918

This volume is one of three Shearsman volumes devoted to Huidobro's publications in 1917 and 1918, all of which appeared soon after his first arrival in Europe and his headlong charge into the avant-garde scene, both in Madrid and, more importantly, in Paris. The other two volumes each contain a single collection: *Horizon carré* (Square Horizon, written in French, although a number of the poems in the first section are adaptations of poems in *El espejo de agua*) and *Poemas árticos* (Arctic Poems, written in Spanish).

This volume includes the remaining publications from that frenetic period and presents, at first glance, an odd mixture. Chronologically, we have *El espejo de agua*, written in 1914-16, first published in 1916, but, to all intents and purposes not distributed until 1918. I say "to all intents and purposes" because almost no-one seems to have seen the 1916 edition in Buenos Aires, which was replicated in the first 1918 print-run. The second 1918 print-run was a reset edition. This is a transitional book, marking the end of the author's involvement with symbolism / *modernismo*—the end of that movement definitively marked by the death in 1916 of its prime mover, Rubén Darío—and his move towards the latest literary fashions in Europe, the latter undoubtedly one of his reasons for uprooting the family from Santiago and moving first to Madrid and then, at the end of 1917, to Paris. (The other reason, and perhaps the prime initial impetus, was the public scandal arising from his affair with Teresa Wilms Montt in Buenos Aires in 1916.) Starting this book with the poem, 'Arte poética', Huidobro may be seen positioning himself for the post-Darío world.

Horizon carré, a large collection, follows and then come *Ecuatorial* (written in Spanish, although the author also made a French version, *Equatoriale*, which appears to be later), *Poemas árticos*, *Hallali* and *Tour Eiffel*, the last two being composed in French. *Tour Eiffel* exists in two versions, one published as a chapbook on coloured paper, with artwork by Robert Delaunay, and another as a contribution to the magazine *Nord-Sud* (also in 1917); it also exists in a Spanish version, made by the author, and published in 1926 in the magazine *Índice*.

After this torrent of publications, Huidobro slowed down, although he published a French-language selected poems, *Saisons choisies*, in Paris in 1921. The next two poetry collections after that were *Automne régulier* and

Tout à coup in 1925, again in French, and significantly different in style, which were to remain the last collections until the astonishing explosion in 1931 represented by *Altazor* (apparently written 1919-1931, with the first magazine publications of parts of the poem occurring in 1925) and *Temblor de cielo* (written 1928). A further poetic silence followed, broken only by two volumes issued in Santiago in 1941, *Ver y palpar, 1923-1933* (Seeing and Feeling) and *El ciudadano del olvido 1924-1934* (The Citizen of Oblivion).

Together with the experimental French poets, Huidobro was also quickly drawn into the group of expatriate Spanish artists—Picasso, Picabia and Juan Gris chief among them. Both Picasso and Gris drew portraits of Huidobro. The cultural ferment in Paris, the war notwithstanding, was something that Huidobro threw himself into. He would soak up the exhibitions, the music—he also got to know Diaghilev, the members of Les Six, and Edgard Varèse—the literary salons and café society. His work was marked by this forever, although he was to calm down in his artistic maturity after the great long works published in 1931. He was also to move into other spheres, leaving some of this poetic experimentation behind, writing novels and stage works, repeatedly founding magazines that quickly folded, while also finding time to join the political fray back in Santiago and, briefly, to run for President.

Like many intellectuals of his era he flirted with leftist politics, and joined the Communist Party—although he was to move away from it decisively in the 1940s. He agitated in Madrid in the late 1930s for the Republican government, against Franco's insurrectionist forces.

Huidobro's personal life also went through its ups and downs. During the early years in Paris he was accompanied by his wife, Manuela Portales—like Vicente, the scion of a Chilean upper-class family, as well as being a descendant of a renowned President—and their children, two born in Chile, and two in Europe. In 1928 he abandoned Manuela in favour of the barely-of-age Ximena Amunátegui, a relative by marriage, whom he whisked away from her boarding school in a dramatic escape to Argentina (with her connivance, it should be added, and the aid of a former family maid), whence the pair went to Paris. The couple had one child, Vicente's last. Vicente had fallen in love with Ximena in 1926, when she was *not* of age, and created an enormous scandal by announcing his infatuation in a long poem that was published in the Santiago newspaper, *La Nación*.

Their marriage lasted officially until 1945, when Ximena requested a divorce; she then married a younger admirer, Godofredo Iommi (1917–2001)—an Argentine poet who had been a great fan of Huidobro's work and had long been besotted with Ximena.

After a stint as a war reporter for Argentine and Uruguayan newspapers in 1944-45, during which he was twice wounded, Huidobro's final years were spent in Cartagena, south of Valparaíso on the Chilean coast, with his third wife, Raquel Señoret, daughter of the Chilean Ambassador to London and previously married to an English writer. He died in Cartagena on 2 January 1948, his end hastened by the deleterious effects of his war wounds.

Further Reading

There are a number of books to be had, but especially useful for the newcomer to the author's work are:

Vicente Huidobro, *Obra poética*, ed. Cedomil Goic (Paris: Eds. ALLCA XX, 2003.

Vicente Huidobro, *Poesía creacionista* [contains *Ecuatorial*, *Poemas árticos* and *Altazor*], ed. Óscar Hahn (Madrid: Visor, 2018)

Enrique Caracciolo Trejo, *La Poesía de Vicente Huidobro y la Vanguardia*. Madrid: Editorial Gredos, 1974.

René de Costa, *Vicente Huidobro: Careers of a Poet*. London: Oxford University Press, 1984.

René de Costa (ed.) *Poesía*. Triple Issue 30, 31 & 32 [a monograph dedicated to the work of Huidobro]. Madrid, 1989.

Volodia Teitelboim, *Huidobro, La marcha infinita*. Santiago: Ediciones BAT, 1993; 2nd edition, Santiago: LOM Ediciones, 2016.

A single-volume edition of *El espejo de agua* and *Ecuatorial* has been published (2012) by Ocho Libros Editores, Santiago, in association with the Fundación Vicente Huidobro. This edition contains only the texts of the poems, and thus those requiring some context or commentary are referred to the Goic collected edition.

A more exhaustive bibliography appears in the *Selected Poems*, also available in this series.

Tony Frazer

EL ESPEJO DE AGUA

A Fernán Félix de Amador, Poeta hermano

MIRROR OF WATER

For Fernán Félix de Amador, brother Poet

ARTE POÉTICA

Que el verso sea como una llave
Que abra mil puertas.
Una hoja cae; algo pasa volando;
Cuanto miren los ojos creado sea,
Y el alma del oyente quede temblando.

Inventa mundos nuevos y cuida tu palabra;
El adjetivo, cuando no da vida, mata.

Estamos en el ciclo de los nervios.
El músculo cuelga,
Como recuerdo, en los museos;
Mas no por eso tenemos menos fuerza:
El vigor verdadero
Reside en la cabeza.

Por qué cantáis la rosa, ¡oh Poetas!
Hacedla florecer en el poema;

Sólo para nosotros
Viven todas las cosas bajo el Sol.

El poeta es un pequeño Dios.

ARS POETICA

Let poetry be like a key
That opens a thousand doors.
A leaf falls; something flies overhead;
Let what the eyes see be created,
And the soul of the listener tremble.

Invent new worlds and watch your word;
The adjective, when it doesn't bring life, kills.

We are in the age of nerves.
Muscles hang,
Like a relic, in museums,
But it doesn't make us weaker:
True strength
Is in the head.

Why sing of the rose, oh Poets?
Make it bloom in the poem.

For us alone
All things live under the Sun.

The Poet is a little God.

EL ESPEJO DE AGUA

Mi espejo, corriente por las noches,
Se hace arroyo y se aleja de mi cuarto.

Mí espejo, más profundo que el orbe
Donde todos los cisnes se ahogaron.

Es un estanque verde en la muralla
Y en medio duerme tu desnudez anclada.

Sobre sus olas, bajo cielos sonámbulos,
Mis ensueños se alejan como barcos.

De pie en la popa siempre me veréis cantando.
Una rosa secreta se hincha en mi pecho
Y un ruiseñor ebrio aletea en mi dedo.

MIRROR OF WATER

My mirror, rushing through the nights,
Forms a stream running off from my room.

My mirror, deeper than the sphere
Where swans drown.

It's a green lake on the wall
Where your anchored naked body sleeps.

Over its waves, under sleepwalking skies,
My dreams send off like ships.

Standing at the stern, you'll see me singing.
A secret rose swells in my chest
And a drunken nightingale flaps on my finger.

EL HOMBRE TRISTE

Lloran voces sobre mi corazón…
No más pensar en nada.
Despierta el recuerdo y el dolor,
Tened cuidado con las puertas mal cerradas.

Las cosas se fatigan.

En la alcoba,
Detrás de la ventana donde el jardín se muere,
Las hojas lloran.

En la chimenea languidece el mundo.

Todo está obscuro,
Nada vive,
Tan sólo en el Ocaso
Brillan los ojos del gato.

Sobre la ruta se alejaba un hombre.

El horizonte habla.
Detrás todo agonizaba.
La madre que murió sin decir nada
Trabaja en mi garganta.

Tu figura se ilumina al fuego
Y algo quiere salir.
El chorro de agua en el jardín.

Alguien tose en la otra pieza,
Una voz vieja.

THE SAD MAN

Voices weep over my heart…
Don't think of anything.
Awaken memories and pain.
Watch out for doors left ajar.

Things get tired.

Outside the bedroom window,
Where the garden is dying,
The leaves weep.

The world languishes in the chimney.

Everything is dark,
Nothing lives,
At nightfall
Only the eyes of the cat shine.

A man has gone off on his way.

The horizon speaks.
Beyond it everything is fading.
The mother who died without saying a word,
Toils on in my throat.

You are lit by the fire
And something wants to leave.
The trickle of water in the garden.

Someone coughs in the other room.
An ancient voice.

¡Cuán lejos!

Un poco de muerte
Tiembla en los rincones.

How far away!

A little bit of death
Trembles in the corner.

EL HOMBRE ALEGRE

No lloverá más,
Pero algunas lágrimas
Brillan aún en tus cabellos.

Un hombre salta en el sol.

Sus ojos llenos del polvo de todos los caminos

Y su canción no brota de sus labios.

El día se rompe contra los vidrios
Y las angustias se desvanecen.

El universo
Es más claro que mi espejo.

El vuelo de los pájaros y el gritar de los niños
Es del mismo color,
                        Verde.
    Sobre los árboles,

Más altos que el cielo,
Se oyen campanas al vuelo.

THE HAPPY MAN

It's stopped raining,
But a few drops
Still shine in your hair.

A man skips in the sun.

His eyes full of the dust from all the roads.

And his song does not spring from his lips.

Day breaks against the windows
And troubles vanish.

The universe
Is clearer than my mirror.

The flight of birds and the shouts of children
Are the same color.
                    Green,
    On the trees.

Higher than the sky,
You can hear the bells flying.

NOCTURNO

Las horas resbalan lentamente
Como las gotas de agua por un vidrio.

Silencio nocturno.

El miedo se esparce por el aire
Y el viento llora en el estanque.

¡Oh!...

Es una hoja.

Se diría que es el fin de las cosas.

Todo el mundo duerme...
Un suspiro;
En la casa alguien ha muerto.

NOCTURNE

The hours slowly trickle
Like drops of water down the window.

Nocturnal silence.

Fear scatters in the air.
And the wind weeps in the pond.

Oh!…

It's a leaf.

It will be said that this is the end of things.

The whole world sleeps…
A sigh;
In the house someone has died.

OTOÑO

Guardo en mis ojos
El calor de tus lágrimas…
Las últimas,
Ya no llorarás más.

Por los caminos
Viene el otoño
Arrancando todas las hojas.

¡Oh qué cansancio!

Una lluvia de alas
Cubre la tierra.

AUTUMN

In my eyes I hold
The heat of your tears...
The last ones.
You won't cry any more.

Autumn comes
Along the roads
Ripping out the leaves.

What exhaustion!

A rain of wings
Covers the earth.

NOCTURNO II

La pieza desierta;
Cerrada está la puerta;
Se siente irse la luz.

Las sombras salen de debajo de los muebles,
Y allá lejos, los objetos perdidos
Se ríen.

La noche.

La alcoba se inunda.
Estoy perdido.
Un grito lleno de angustia;
Nadie ha respondido.

NOCTURNE II

    The empty room:
The closed door;
It feels like the light has gone.

    Shadows escape from under the furniture,
And there, far off, things that were lost
Laugh.

Night.

The bedroom is flooded.
I'm lost.
A cry of distress;
No one answers.

AÑO NUEVO

El sueño de Jacob se ha realizado;
Un ojo se abre frente al espejo
Y las gentes que bajan a la tela
Arrojaron su carne como un abrigo viejo.

La película mil novecientos dieciséis
Sale de una caja.

La guerra europea.

Llueve sobre los espectadores
Y hay un ruido de temblores.

Hace frío.

Detrás de la sala
Un viejo ha rodado al vacío.

NEW YEAR

Jacob's dream has come true;
An eye opens in front of a mirror
And the people lowering the screen
Throw off their flesh like an old coat.

The movie 1916
Comes out of the box.

The European War.

Rain on the spectators
And a rumble of tremors.

It's cold.

At the back of the auditorium
An old man has wheeled into the void.

ALGUIEN IBA A NACER

Algo roza los muros…
Un alma quiere nacer.

Ciega aún.

Alguien busca una puerta,
Mañana sus ojos mirarán.

Un ruido se ahoga en los tapices.

¿Todavía no encuentras?

Pues bien, vete,
No vengas.

En la vida
Sólo a veces hay un poco de sol.

Sin embargo vendrá,
Alguien la espera.

SOMEONE WAS
GOING TO BE BORN

Something brushes against the walls…
A soul wants to be born.

Still blind.

Someone looks for a door,
Tomorrow his eyes will see.

A sound muffled in the upholstery.

You still can't find it?

So go then,
Don't come.

In life
Only sometimes is there a little sun.

Nevertheless it will come.
Someone is waiting.

ECUATORIAL

EQUATORIAL

for Pablo Picasso

Era el tiempo en que se abrieron mis párpados sin alas
Y empecé a cantar sobre las lejanías desatadas

Saliendo de sus nidos
                        Atruenan el aire las banderas

LOS HOMBRES
            ENTRE LA YERBA
                        BUSCABAN LAS FRONTERAS
Sobre el campo banal
                        el mundo muere
De las cabezas prematuras
                                brotan las alas ardientes
Y en la trinchera ecuatorial
                        trizada a trechos

Bajo la sombra de aeroplanos vivos
Los soldados cantaban en las tardes duras

Las ciudades de Europa
                        Se apagan una a una

Caminando al destierro
El último rey portaba al cuello
Una cadena de lámparas extintas

                Las estrellas
                        que caían
                Eran luciérnagas del musgo

Y los afiches ahorcados
                        pendían a lo largo de los muros

It was the time when my eyelids opened still wingless
And I began to sing of far-off places unraveling

Leaving their nests
                                        Flags stun the air

MEN
            LOOKED FOR THE BORDERLINES
                                                IN THE GRASS
The world dies
                        on an ordinary field
Immature heads
                                    sprout flaming wings
Along the smashed stretches
                                of the equatorial trench

Under the shadows of the vivacious aeroplanes
Soldiers were singing in the hard afternoons

The cities of Europe
                        Go out one by one

Walking into exile
The last king wore a chain
Of extinguished lanterns around his neck

                    The stars
                                that fell
                Were glowworms of moss

And posters were hanged
                                along the walls

Una sombra rodó sobre la falda de los montes
Donde el viejo organista hace cantar las selvas

El viento mece los horizontes
Colgados de las jarcias y las velas

Sobre el arco-iris
Un pájaro cantaba

Abridme la montaña

Por todas partes en el suelo
He visto alas de golondrinas
Y el cristo que alzó el vuelo
Dejó olvidada la corona de espinas

Sentados sobre el paralelo
Miremos nuestro tiempo

SIGLO ENCADENADO EN UN ANGULO DEL MUNDO

En los espejos corrientes
Pasan las barcas bajo los puentes
Y los ángeles-correo
Reposan en el humo de los dreadnought

Entre la hierba
silba la locomotora en celo
Que atravesó el invierno
Las dos cuerdas de su rastro
Tras ella quedan cantando
Como una guitarra indócil

Su ojo desnudo
Cigarro del horizonte
Danza entre los árboles

Ella es el diógenes con la pipa encendida
Buscando entre los meses y los días

A shadow circled over the foothills
Where the ancient organist makes the forest sing

        Wind rocks horizons
        Lifted by rigging and sails

A bird sang
            Over the rainbow

        Open the mountain for me

I saw the wings of swallows
Scattered on the ground
And Christ took flight
And forgot to take his crown of thorns

        Sitting above the parallel line
        We look at our age

CENTURY CHAINED TO A CORNER OF THE WORLD

In the mirrors of the present
Boats go by under the bridges
And angel-postmen
           Rest in the smoke of the dreadnoughts

In the grass
          the locomotive that crossed the winter
Whistles in heat
The two strings of its track
Still singing
Like an untamed guitar

Its naked eye
        Cigar of the horizon
                Dances in the trees

It's Diogenes with a lit pipe
Searching among the months and days

Sobre el sendero equinoccial
Empecé a caminar

Cada estrella
                    Es un obús que estalla

Las plumas de mi garganta
Se entibiaron al sol
                              que perdió un ala

El divino aeroplano
Traía un ramo de olivo entre las manos

Sin embargo
                    Los ocasos heridos se desengran
Y en el puerto los días que se alejan
Llevaban una cruz en el sitio del ancla

Cantando nos sentamos en las playas

Los más bravos capitanes   El capitán Cook
En un iceberg iban a los polos   Caza aurora boreales
Para dejar su pipa en labios   En el polo sur
Esquimales

Otros clavan frescas lanzas en el Congo

El corazón del África soleado
Se abre como los higos picoteados

Y los negros
                    de divina raza
esclavos en Europa
Limpiando de su rostro
                              la nieve que los mancha

Hombres de alas cortas
                              Han recorrido todo
Y un noble explorador de la Noruega

I began to walk
Along the equinoctial path

Every star
           A bursting shell

The feathers of my throat
Cooled by the sun
                    that had lost a wing

The divine aeroplane
Brought an olive branch in its hands

And yet
           Wounded sunsets are still bleeding
And the days set off from the harbor
Carrying a cross instead of an anchor

We sit singing on the beaches

The most courageous captains   Captain Cook
Left on an iceberg to the poles   Hunts aurora borealises
To stick their pipes   At the South Pole
In Eskimo lips

Others plant fresh lances in the Congo

The sunstruck heart of Africa
Opens like pecked figs

And Negroes
           of the divine race
slaves in Europe
Washed off the snow
                    that stained their faces

Men with clipped wings
                  Have overrun everything
And a noble explorer from Norway

Como botín de guerra
Trajo de Europa
                          entre raros animales
Y árboles exóticos
Los cuatro puntos cardinales

Yo he embarcado también
Dejando mi arrecife vine a veros

Las gaviotas volaban en torno a mi sombrero

Y heme aquí
                de pie
                          en otras bahías

Bajo el boscaje afónico
Pasan lentamente
                          las ciudades cautivas
Cosidas una a una por hilos telefónicos

Y las palabras y los gestos
Vuelan en torno del telégrafo
Quemando las alas
                          cual dioses inexpertos

Los aeroplanos fatigados
Iban a posarse sobre los para-rayos
Biplanos encinta
                          pariendo al vuelo entre la niebla

Son los pájaros amados
Que en nuestras jaulas han cantado

Es el pájaro que duerme entre las ramas
Sin cubrir la cabeza bajo el ala

En las noches
                          los aviones volaban junto al faro
El faro que agoniza al fondo de los años

Brought back to Europe
As the spoils of war
                Along with the rare animals
And exotic trees
The four cardinal points

And I too have embarked
Leaving my reef I came to see you

Seagulls flew around my hat

And here I am
              standing
                            in other bays

Under the voiceless trees
The captive cities
                slowly go by
Sewn to one another by telephone wires

And words and faces
Fly around the telegraph
Burning their wings
                    like inexperienced gods

Exhausted aeroplanes
Went off to rest on the lightning rods
Biplanes in labor
                        give birth flying through the fog

They are the love birds
That sang in our cages

The bird that sleeps in the branches
Without tucking its head under its wing

At night
                    the planes flew by the lighthouse
The lighthouse dying at the end of the years

Alguien amargado
                              Las pupilas vacías
Lanzando al mar sus tristes días
Toma el barco

Partir
                    Y de allá lejos
Mirar las ventanas encendidas
Y las sombras que cruzan los espejos

Como una bandada
                              de golondrinas jóvenes
Los emigrantes cantaban sobre las olas invertidas

                                        M A R

MAR DE HUMAREDAS VERDES

Yo querría ese mar para mi sed de antaño
Lleno de flotantes cabelleras

Sobre esas olas fuéronse mis ansias verdaderas

Bajo las aguas gaseosas
                                        Un serafín náufrago
                                        Teje coronas de algas

La luna nueva
                        con las jarcias rotas
Ancló en Marsella esta mañana

Y los más viejos marineros
En el fondo del humo de sus pipas
Habían encontrado perlas vivas

El capitán del submarino
Olvidó en el fondo su destino

Al volver a la tierra
                              Vio que otro llevaba su estrella

Someone embittered
                              Empty eyes
Takes a boat
Casting his sad days into the sea

To leave
                    And from there far-off
To see the lit windows
And the shadows that cross the mirrors

Like a flock
                              of young swallows
Emigrants were singing on the inverted waves

                                        S E A

SEA OF GREEN CLOUDS OF SMOKE

I wanted that sea for my old thirst
Full of floating strands of hair

On those waves they were my true desires

Under the gaseous water
                                        A shipwrecked seraphim
                                        Weaves crowns of seaweed

The new moon
                              with its rigging broken
Anchored in Marseilles this morning

And the most ancient sailors
Found living pearls
At the bottom of their pipe smoke

The submarine captain
In the depths forgot his mission

Returning to land
                              He saw that someone else was wearing his star

Desterrados fiebrosos del planeta viejo
Muerto al alzar el vuelo
Por los cañones antiaéreos

Un emigrante ciego
                        Traía cuatro leones amaestrados
Y otro llevaba al hospital del puerto
Un ruiseñor desafinado

Aquel piloto niño
                        que olvidó su pipa humeante
Junto al volcán extinto
Encontró en la ciudad
                        los hombres de rodillas
Y vio alumbrar las vírgenes encinta

Allá lejos
                        Allá lejos

Vienen pensativos
                        los buscadores de oro

Pasan cantando entre las hojas
Sobre sus hombros
Traen la California

Al fondo del crepúsculo
Venían los mendigos semimudos

Un rezador murmullo
                        Inclinaba los árboles

                Sobre los mares
                Huyó el Estío

QUÉ DE COSAS HE VISTO

Entre la niebla vegetal y espesa
Los mendigos de las calles de Londres

Feverish exiles from the old planet
That was killed on take-off
By anti-aircraft guns

A blind emigrant
                                        Brought four trained lions
And another took a nightingale that was out of tune
To the harbor hospital

That boy pilot
                        who left his smoking pipe
Near the extinct volcano
Found men on their knees
                                in the city
And saw pregnant virgins giving birth

There far-off
                                                There far-off

Pensive gold prospectors come
                        Singing among the leaves

Carrying California
On their shoulders

Half-mute beggars came
Through the depths of twilight

The murmur of someone praying
                                Bowed the trees over

                Summertime fled
                Over the seas

WHAT THINGS I'VE SEEN

In the thick and vegetal fog
Beggars on the streets of London

Pegados como anuncios
Contra los fríos muros

Recuerdo bien
                    Recuerdo

Aquella tarde en Primavera
Una muchacha enferma
Dejando sus dos alas a la puerta
Entraba al sanatorio

Aquella misma noche
                              bajo el cielo oblongo
Diez Zeppelines vinieron a París
Y un cazador de jabalís
Dejó sangrando siete
Sobre el alba agreste

Entre la nube que rozaba el techo

Un reloj verde

                    Anuncia el año

1917

LLUEVE

                                        Bajo el agua
                                        Enterraban los muertos

                    Alguien que lloraba
                    Hacía caer las hojas

Signos hay en el cielo
Dice el astrólogo barbudo
                                        Una manzana y una estrella
                                        Picotean los búhos

46

Stuck like posters
Against the frigid walls

I remember it well
                    I remember

That afternoon in Spring
A girl who was ill
Left her two wings at the door
And went into the sanatorium

That same night
                              under the oblong sky
Ten Zeppelins arrived in Paris
And a hunter of wild boars
Left seven bleeding
In the country dawn

In the cloud that brushes the roof

A green clock

                    Announces the year

1917

IT'S RAINING

                                        They buried the dead
                                        Underwater

                    Someone weeping
                    Made the leaves fall

There are signs in the sky
Says the bearded astrologer

                                        Owls are pecking
                                        An apple and a star

Marte
        pasa a través de
                Sagitario

SALE LA LUNA

            Un astro maltratado
            Se desliza

Astrólogos de mitras puntiagudas
De sus barbas caían copos de ceniza

Y heme aquí
        Entre las selvas afinadas
Más sabiamente que las viejas arpas

En la casa
       que cuelga del vacío
Cansados de buscar
           los Reyes Magos se han dormido

Los ascensores descansan en cuclillas

Y en todas las alcobas
Cada vez que da la hora
Salía del reloj un paje serio
Como a decir
        El coche aguarda
            mi señora

Junto a la puerta viva
El negro esclavo
        abre la boca prestamente
Para el amo pianista
Que hace cantar sus dientes

Esta tarde yo he visto
Los últimos afiches fonográficos
Era una confusión de gritos

Mars

        passes through

                Sagittarius

THE MOON COMES OUT

            A mistreated star
            Slips away

Flakes of ashes fell from the beards
Of astrologers in pointy miters

And here I am
        In forests
More expertly tuned than old harps

In the house
        that hangs in the void
Tired of searching
              the Three Kings have gone to sleep

Elevators squatting doze

And in every bedroom
When it strikes the hour
A reliable bellhop comes out of the clock
As if to say
        The car is waiting
              Madam

Next to the open door
The negro slave
           quickly opens his mouth
For the master pianist
Who can make his teeth sing

This afternoon I've seen
The latest phonographic notices
A riot of screams

Y cantos tan diversos
Como en los puertos extranjeros

Los hombres de mañana
Vendrán a descifrar los jeroglíficos
Que dejamos ahora
Escritos al revés
Entre los hierros de la Torre Eiffel

Llegamos al final de la refriega
Mi reloj perdió todas sus horas

Yo te recorro lentamente
Siglo cortado en dos
                              Y con un puente
Sobre un río sangriento
Camino de Occidente

Una tarde
                    al fondo de la vida
Pasaba un horizonte de camellos
En sus espaldas mudas
Entre dos pirámides huesudas
Los hombres del Egipto
Lloran como los nuevos cocodrilos

Y los santos en tren
                                      buscando otras regiones
Bajaban y subían en todas las estaciones

Mi alma hermana de los trenes

                              Un tren puede rezarse como un rosario
                              La cruz humeante perfumaba los llanos

Henos aquí viajando entre los santos

El tren es un trozo de la ciudad que se aleja

And songs as sundry
As those in foreign ports

The men of tomorrow
Will decipher the hieroglyphs
We've left
Written backwards
On the girders of the Eiffel Tower

We've reached the end of the skirmish
My watch lost its time

I travel slowly through you
Century cut in half
                              And on a bridge
Over a bloody river
I walk from the West

One afternoon
                    deep in life
A horizon of camels passed by
On their mute backs
Between two bony pyramids
The men of Egypt
Weep like newborn crocodiles

On the train the saints
                              looking for other territories
Get on and off at every station

My sister soul of the trains

            A train can pray to itself like a rosary
            The smoking cross that perfumed the plains

Here we are traveling with saints

A train is a piece of the city that pushes off

El anunciador de estaciones
Ha gritado

                Primavera
                Al lado izquierdo
                    30 minutos

Pasa el tren lleno de flores y de frutos

El Niágara ha mojado mis cabellos
Y una neblina nace en torno de ellos

Los ríos
                Todos los ríos de las nacientes cabelleras
Los ríos mal trenzados
Que los ardientes veranos han besado

Un paquebot perdido costeaba
Las islas de oro de la Vía Láctea

La cordillera Andina
                      Veloz como un convoy
Atraviesa la América Latina.

El Amor

                          El Amor

En pocos sitios lo he encontrado
Y todos los ríos no explorados
Bajo mis brazos han pasado

Una mañana
                Tocaban el violín sobre la Suiza
Pastores alpinistas

Y en la estrella vecina
Aquel que no tenía manos
Con las alas tocaba el piano
Siglo embarcado en aeroplanos ebrios

                    A DONDE IRÁS

The conductor
Shouted

                    Spring
                    Exit on the left
                          30 minutes

The train goes by full of flowers and fruit

Niagara Falls has drenched my hair
And a mist rises around it

The rivers
                    All the rivers of rising hair
The badly braided rivers
That burning summers have kissed

A lost steamer was coasting along
The golden islands of the Milky Way

The Andes mountains
                    Swift as a convoy
Crosses Latin America

Love

                              Love

In few places I've found it
All the unexplored rivers
Have passed beneath my hands

One morning
                    Mountaineer shepherds
Played the violin over Switzerland

And on the star next door
The one who had no hands
Played the piano with his wings
Century embarked on drunken aeroplanes

                    WHERE ARE YOU GOING

Caminando al destierro
El último rey portaba al cuello
Una cadena de Lámparas extintas

Y ayer vi muerta entre las rosas
La amatista de Roma

ALFA

           OMEGA

     DILUVIO

              ARCO IRIS

Cuántas veces la vida habrá recomendado

Quién dirá todo lo que en un astro ha pasado

     Sigamos nuestra marcha
     Llevando la cabeza madura entre las manos

EL RUISEÑOR MECÁNICO HA CANTADO

Aquella multitud de manos ásperas
Lleva coronas funerarias
Hacia los campos de batalla

     Alguien pasó perdido en su cigarro

     QUIÉN ES

Una mano cortada
Dejó sobre los mármoles
La línea Ecuatorial recién brotada

Siglo
     Sumérgete en el sol

Walking into exile
The last king wore a chain of extinguished lanterns
Around his neck

And yesterday I saw the amethyst of Rome
Dead among the roses

ALPHA

                    OMEGA

          FLOOD

                              RAINBOW

How many times will life have to begin again

Who will tell everything that has happened on a star

                    We continue our march
                    Carrying the ripened head in our hands

THE MECHANICAL NIGHTINGALE HAS SUNG

That throng of rough hands
Carrying funeral wreaths
To the battlefields

          Someone went by lost in his cigar

                    WHO IS IT

A severed hand
Left the new equatorial line
On the marble

Century
          Sink into the sun

Cuando en la tarde
        Aterrice en un campo de aviación

Hacía el solo aeroplano
Que cantará un día en el azul
Se alzará de los altos
Una bandada de manos

CRUZ DEL SUR

SUPREMO SIGNO   AVIÓN DE CRISTO

El niño sonrosado de las alas desnudas
Vendrá con el clarín entre dedos
El clarín aún fresco que anuncia
El Fin del Universo

When in the evening
          It lands at the airfield

A flock of hands
Will rise from the years
Toward the one aeroplane
That will sing someday in the blue

                THE SOUTHERN CROSS

THE SUPREME SIGN   THE CHRIST AIRLINER

The rosy child with bare wings
Will come with his bugle in his hands
The brand-new bugle that heralds
The End of the Universe

HALLALI

poème de guerre

A mon ami Marius André

HALLALI

a poem of the war

For my friend Marius André

1914

Nuages sur le jet d'eau d'été
    La nuit
        Toutes les tours de l'Europe se parlaient en secret

Tout d'un coup un œil s'ouvre
La corne de la lune crie

Hallali
                       Hallali
Les tours sont des clairons pendus

AOÛT 1914
          C'est la vendange des frontières

Derrière l'horizon il se passe quelque chose

        Au gibet de l'Aurore toutes les villes sont pendues
          Les villes qui fument comme des pipes

Hallali
                       Hallali
Et ce n'est pas une chanson
                Les hommes s'en vont

1914

Clouds over the fountain of summer
    Night
                All the towers of Europe trading secrets

Suddenly an eye opens
The horn of the moon blasts

Hallali
                                Hallali
The towers are bugles swinging

AUGUST 1914
                    A vintage year for frontiers

Something's happening beyond the horizon

            All the cities swinging from the gallows of dawn
                The cities smoking like pipes

Hallali
                                Hallali
And it's not a song
                        The men go off

LES VILLES

Dans les villes
On parle
          On parle
Mais on ne dit rien

La terre nue roule encore
Et même les pierres crient

Soldats vêtus de nuages bleues
                    Le ciel vieilli entre les mains
                    Et la chanson dans la tranchée

Les trains s'en vont sur des cordes parallèles

                    On pleure dans toutes les gares

Le premier tué a été un poète
On a vu un oiseau s'échapper de sa blessure

L'aéroplane blanc de neige
Gronde parmi les colombes du soir

Un jour
        il s'était égaré dans la fumée des cigares

     Nuées des usines   Nuées du ciel

          C'est un trompe-l'œil

THE CITIES

In the cities
They talk
        They talk
And don't say a thing

The bare earth still turns
And even the rocks cry

Soldiers dressed in blue clouds
                   The sky grows old between their hands
                   And the song in the trenches

The trains go off on their parallel ropes

                   There's weeping at every station

The first to be killed was a poet
A bird was seen flying from his wound

An aeroplane white as snow
Roars through the evening doves

One day
        it was got lost in the smoke of cigars

    The haze of the factories   The haze of the sky

          It's a trompe-l'œil

Les blessures des aviateurs saignent dans toutes les étoiles

Un cri d'angoisse
S'est noyé dans les brouillards
Et un enfant à genoux
Lève les mains

TOUTES LES MÈRES DU MONDE PLEURENT

The wounds of aviators bleed over the stars

A cry of pain
Drowns in the mist
And a child on his knees
                    Lifts his hands

            ALL THE MOTHERS OF THE WORLD WEEP

LA TRANCHÉE

Sur le canon
Un rossignol chantait

        J'ai perdu mon violon
La tranchée
Fait le tour de la Terre
        Quel froid
            Tous les pères habillés en soldats

On siffle derrière sa propre vie

CRAONNE
        VERDUN
               ALSACE

        C'est une belle cible la lune

L'ombre d'un soldat
Etait tombée dans un trou

    On voit par terre sanglant
    L'aviateur qui se cogna la tête contre une étoile éteinte

Et mieux qu'un chien
Le canon surveille
        Quelques fois
        Il aboie
            LA LUNE

Toutes les étoiles sont des trous d'obus

THE TRENCH

On the cannon
A nightingale sang

        I've lost my violin

The trench
Goes around the world

            It's so cold

                    Every father dressed like a soldier

Whistling for his life

CRAONNE

             VERDUN

                        ALSACE

                What a lovely target is the moon

The shadow of a soldier
Fallen into a pit

    Seen on the bloody ground
    An aviator who smashed his head on a burnt-out star

Better than a dog
The cannon keeps watch

             Sometimes
             Howling

                  THE MOON

Every star a shell hole

LE CIMETIÈRE DES SOLDATS

L'ombre qui tombe des arbres
S'est mouillée dans l'eau

        On ne voit pas le vent

                Mais la forêt métallique
                Chante comme un orgue

La voilà
      La France d'hier sous l'herbe
      Plus belle qu'une femme nue

La terre encore tiède
Garde les derniers secrets

      Où sont toutes les mains coupées

Une cloche sonne
Derrière les nuages

                Tournée vers l'océan filial
                Elle appelait quelqu'un

SILENCE

                SILENCE

SOLDIERS' CEMETERY

The shadow that falls from the trees
Is drenched in the water

      The wind can't be seen

            But the forest of metal
            Sings like an organ

There it is
      The France of yesterday under grass
      More beautiful than a naked woman

The earth still warm
Guards its last secrets

      Where the severed hands all are

A clock strikes
Behind the clouds

            Facing the filial ocean
            It calls out to someone

SILENCE

            SILENCE

LE JOUR DE LA VICTOIRE

Un jour la Paix viendra

                                            Torche au fond du siècle

Alors les soldats   les yeux pleins de pluie

Regagneront Paris

     UN OISEAU CHANTERA SUR L'ARC DE TRIOMPHE

Et le retour

Éclairera toutes les fenêtres

Avions

                      Soldats

                                            Canons

Même les aveugles

Sortiront aux balcons

Et leurs fleurs tomberont aussi sur les têtes des soldats

Le cortège viendra des siècles plus lointains

La foule dansera dans les yeux des chevaux

          Un cri s'élève comme une étincelle

          Et les chapeaux monteront dans l'air

          Mieux que les houles dans les jets d'eaux

Avions

                      Soldats

                                            Canons

THE DAY OF VICTORY

One day Peace will come

                                    Torchlight in the depths of the century

And the soldiers   eyes full of rain

Will go back to Paris

    A BIRD WILL SING ON THE ARC DE TRIOMPHE

And homecoming

Will light the windows

Planes

                                Soldiers

                                                            Cannons

Even the blind

Will come out on the balconies

And their flowers too will fall on the heads of soldiers

The cortège will come from distant ages

The crowds will dance in the horses' eyes

                A shout will go up like a flash of light

                And hats will shoot into the air

                Like the balls at the tip of a fountain

Planes

                                Soldiers

                                                                Cannons

LES AÉROPLANES   LES AÉROPLANES

Ne fermeront pas leurs ailes tout ce matin

LES AÉROPLANES   LES AÉROPLANES

De quel cimetière de héros
Sont envolées ces croix
Chanter la gloire de leurs morts

Le jour de la Victoire
Tous les peuples chanteront

Et les mers
Se changeront en miel

Soldats

Canons

Un ballon jette un bouquet de fleurs

Les matelots lointains

Les matelots couleur de vieille pipe

Chanteront à genoux sur les vagues

La Seine coulera pleine de fleurs
Et ses ponts
Seront aussi des arcs de triomphe

AEROPLANES   AEROPLANES

Won't fold their wings that morning

AEROPLANES   AEROPLANES

From which cemetery of heroes
Have these crosses flown
Singing the glory of their dead

                              Victory Day
                              Everyone will sing

                              And the seas
                              Will turn into honey

Soldiers

                    Cannons

            A balloon throws out a bouquet of flowers

The far-off sailors

                                        Sailors the color of old pipes

            Will sing on their knees over the waves

The Seine will flow by full of flowers
And its bridges too
Will be arches of triumph

LES VILLES ET LES TAMBOURS ROULENT

Et quand la nuit viendra
Les étoiles tomberont sur la foule

Et après
Tout en haut de la Tour Eiffel
J'allume mon cigare
                    Pour les astres en danger

Là-bas
            Sur la borne du monde
Quelqu'un chante un hymne de triomphe

And when night comes
Stars will fall on the crowds

And then
At the top of the Eiffel Tower
I'll light my cigar
                    For the threatened stars

Down there
                    At the end of the earth
Someone's singing a triumphal hymn

TOUR EIFFEL

à Robert Delaunay

EIFFEL TOWER

for Robert Delaunay

Le Tour 1910 — PARIS

DELAUNAY

Tour Eiffel
Guitare du ciel

        Ta télégraphie sans fil
        Attire les mots
        Comme un rosier les abeilles

Pendant la nuit
La Seine ne coule plus

        Télescope ou clairon

        TOUR EIFFEL

Et c'est une ruche de mots
Ou un encrier de miel

Tour Eiffel
Guitare du ciel
Guitar of the sky

> Attracting words
> To your telegraphy
> Like a rosebush its bees

At night
The Seine stops flowing

> Telescope or bugle

> EIFFEL TOWER

It's a hive of words
An inkwell of honey

Au fond de l'aube
Une araignée aux pattes en fil de fer
Faisait sa toile de nuages

       Mon petit garçon
       Pour monter à la Tour Eiffel
       On monte sur un chanson

       Do
             ré
                  mi
                       fa
                            sol
                                 la
                                      si
                                         do

          Nous sommes en haut

Un oiseau chante   C'est le vent
Dans les antennes   De l'Europe
Télégraphiques   Le vent électrique

          Là-bas

Les chapeaux s'envolent
Ils ont des ailes mais ils ne chantent pas

At the end of dawn
A spider with wire legs
Spun a web of clouds

    My boy
    To climb the Eiffel Tower
    You climb up on a song

    Do
        ré
            mi
                fa
                    sol
                        la
                          si
                            do

    Nous sommes en haut
     We're at the top

A bird sings   It's the wind
In the telegraph   Of Europe
Antennas   The electric wind

    Down there

Hats fly off
They have wings but can't sing

Jacqueline
            Fille de France
Qu'est-ce que tu vois là-haut

La Seine dort
Sous l'ombre de ses ponts

Je vois tourner la Terre
Et je sonne mon clairon
Vers toutes les mers

            Sur le chemin
            De ton parfum
            Tous les abeilles et les paroles s'en vont

            Sur les quatre horizons
Qui n'a pas entendu cette chanson

JE SUIS LE REINE DE L'AUBE DE PÔLES
JE SUIS LA ROSE DES VENTS QUI SE FANE TOUS LES AUTOMNES
ET TOUTE PLEINE DE NEIGE
JE MEURS DE LA MORT DE CETTE ROSE
DANS ME TÊTE UN OISEAU CHANTE TOUTE L'ANNÉE

C'est comme ça qu'un jour la Tour m'a parlé

Jacqueline
               Daughter of France
What do you see up there?

The Seine's asleep
Under the shadow of its bridges

I can see the Earth turning
And I blow my bugle
To all the seas

        On the road
        Of your perfume
        All the bees and all the words take off

        On the four horizons
Who hasn't heard this song

I AM THE QUEEN OF THE DAWN OF THE POLES
I AM THE COMPASS ROSE OF THE WINDS THAT FADES EVERY FALL
AND FILLED WITH SNOW
I DIE FROM THE DEATH OF THAT ROSE
ALL YEAR LONG A BIRD SINGS INSIDE MY HEAD

That's how the Tower spoke to me one day

Tour Eiffel
Volière du monde

        Chante   Chante

Sonnerie de Paris

Le géant pendu au milieu du vide
Est l'affiche de France

        Le jour de la Victoire
        Tu la raconteras aux étoiles

Paris Août 1917.

Eiffel Tower
Aviary of the world

       Sing   Sing

Bell-clang of Paris

The giant hanging in the void
Is a poster for France

        On the day of Victory
        You'll tell it to the stars

Paris August 1917.

NOTES

El espejo de agua. Poemas 1915-1916

This chapbook was published by Biblioteca Orión in Buenos Aires in 1916, before Huidobro's arrival in Europe, and only a couple of copies of that edition seem to have survived, which are now in the possession of the Fundación Huidobro, having been previously in the hands of the author in one case, and his eldest daughter in the other. This edition was superseded by a second edition in Madrid in 1918, identical with its predecessor in all respects, but with no publisher listed; this was apparently printed for the author by Imprenta Jesús López. There is a note in the Huidobro papers, signed by Tomás Mariñas, director of the firm, to the effect that he had printed the second edition in June 1918 "exactamente igual al ejemplar de la primera edición del mismo libro, publicado in Buenos Aires y traído aquí como modelo por el Sr. Huidobro" [*exactly the same as the copy of the first edition of the same book, published in Buenos Aires and brought here as a master copy by Mr Huidobro*][1] A third edition, reset, appeared later the same year.

There was a furore at one time over the veracity (or otherwise) of the Argentinian edition, with an accusation being made that Huidobro had antedated the information in the Madrid edition, in order to lay claim to being the founder of Creationism. Pierre Reverdy likewise claimed some responsibility for that movement's founding and the two poets, previously friends, fell out over the affair. Orión had also published an edition of Huidobro's earlier collection, *Adán*. Scholarship today is on Huidobro's side, thanks to the evidence described above, but the whole incident was a decidedly minor hiccup in literary history, even if it did lead to Reverdy and Huidobro ending their friendship. *El espejo de agua* is clearly a transitional work, in a different style to that employed in *Adán*, but not as radical as the work to follow in the other publications from 1917 and 1918.

Five of the poems in the book were translated into French, with the extensive help of others (if not *entirely* by others), and published in 1917 in the magazine *Nord-Sud*: 'El hombre triste' (manuscripts suggest that this was in fact entirely Reverdy's work), 'Otoño', 'Nocturno', 'Nocturno II' and 'Alguien iba a nacer'. These and two more then appeared in the

---

[1] Vicente Huidobro, *Obra poética*, ed. Cedomil Goic, Paris: ALLCA, 2003, p.384

volume *Horizon carré* [also available in this series of Shearsman editions], while the poem 'El espejo de agua' was to appear in French in *Saisons choisies*, a selected poems in French, in 1921, thus leaving only 'Arte poética' unpublished in French translation.

Ecuatorial

This poem was written in March/April 1918 and was published in August of the same year by Imprenta Juan Pueyo, Madrid, as a limited-edition chapbook. The entire text was then reprinted in the Madrid magazine *Cervantes* in July 1919. The formatting of the latter version was however reduced and the text contained a number of errors. A second separate edition only appeared in 1978 in Santiago, edited by Óscar Hahn, and was based on the Spanish edition, although the text had also been reprinted in the interim in two separate collected editions of Huidobro's work

There is a French version in manuscript of the first 81 lines, which appears to be in the hand of Picasso, while another exists of the complete poem, but lacking the spatial elements of the first edition. This was not published until the 2003 *Obra poética*, albeit being re-set there to accord with the layout of the Spanish version.

Hallali

This chapbook was published in Madrid by Imprenta Jesús López in 1918. A Spanish version of the complete text appeared in the magazine *Cervantes* in August 1919, an issue which also includes the manifesto of Ultraism, the latest avant-garde movement, and one which was influenced by Huidobro's example; Gerardo Diego and Juan Larrea, both close friends of Huidobro, were amongst that movement's early adherents, as was, for a short time, Jorge Luis Borges, then a resident of Madrid.

Hallali – the word exists in both French and English – is the bugle signal to advance, used for the cavalry, mounted hunters and, here, foot soldiers in the trenches.

Tour Eiffel

Tour Eiffel first appeared in a more traditional left-adjusted layout in Reverdy's magazine *Nord-Sud* in the August-September 1917 issue, with a dedication to Max Jacob. It then appeared as a splendid chapbook in

Madrid in 1918, published by Imprenta Juan Pueyo, where it gained its current spatialised layout. This edition also benefited from coloured pages, a cover image by Robert Delaunay (now the dedicatee of the poem) and a tipped-in reproduction of Delaunay's painting *La Tour*, of 1910, which we have reproduced here on the section title.

Copies of the chapbook are in a number of art galleries, and a (*not entirely* accurate) facsimile was included as an insert with the special Huidobro issue of *Poesía*, edited by René de Costa, triple issue 30, 31 & 32, Madrid, 1989. The latter is indispensable for admirers of Huidobro's work.

A scan of the first edition may be downloaded as a PDF from the Museo Vicente Huidobro in Cartagena: http://www.museovicentehuidobro.cl/documentos/TOUR-EIFFEL-TORRE-EIFFEL.pdf

Tony Frazer

The Translator

Eliot Weinberger's books of literary essays include *Karmic Traces, An Elemental Thing*, and *The Ghosts of Birds*. His political articles are collected in *What I Heard About Iraq* and *What Happened Here: Bush Chronicles*. The author of *19 Ways of Looking at Wang Wei*, he is a translator of the poetry of Bei Dao, the editor of *The New Directions Anthology of Classical Chinese Poetry*, and the general editor of the series *Calligrams: Writings from and on China*. Among his translations of Latin American literature are *The Poems of Octavio Paz*, Jorge Luis Borges' *Selected Non-Fictions*, Vicente Huidobro's *Altazor*, and Xavier Villaurrutia's *Nostalgia for Death*. His work regularly appears in the *London Review of Books* and has been translated into over thirty languages.

Lightning Source UK Ltd.
Milton Keynes UK
UKHW041828130319
339059UK00001B/167/P